EAST 17

WORD UP

TONY MORTIMER

Who are East 17? What's it all about? How did we get here? Questions, questions; we've been asked 'em all, and answered most of 'em. So, we ain't gonna waste your time or ours by bunging out a book full of the same old, tired bull. Instead, we're gonna do this thing with a bit of style, apply our minds and... just tell it like it is. And was. Here's the plot. Walthamstow. One bloke, skinny in flesh but fat with ideas, hoped and dreamed and schemed for the chance to spread his word through music. Peace, Love and Understanding. His name is Tony. A friend of his, with as many muscles as he had girls wanting to squeeze them, heard where his mate was coming from and jumped down from the roofs where he had been slapping up tiles. His name is John. Then this quiet, moody type - with teeth knocked back in a fight so he doesn't like smiling much - got the call and knew he could dance his dance to it. He even managed a grin. His name is Terry. Last, but not least, a small geezer, all mouth with trousers to match, bragged to the others that he could sing with as much suss and savvy as he could talk. And he could. His name is Brian. What else do you want to know? We're East 17. We're an average bunch of blokes from a town like yours and we make music. We sing, we dance. We like clothes, cars, cash. We love women. Anyone could be us, we reckon, but they ain't...

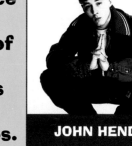

JOHN HENDY

TERRY COLDWELL

BRIAN HARVEY

DOGGY STYLE

In the beginning there was the idea, and the idea was good: make a mark, make a statement and make people remember it. Give them a clue so they can get the picture. Mickey Mouse, Batman... Bob Dog. Just say the words and you see the image. Strong, cool, doggy style. We called him Bob because, well, we called each other Bob around the time he was invented. Bob's your Uncle. Bob also identified with our 'fifth' member, Levy, but he represented all of us, too. Our designers played around with the logo, customised it, individualised it.

It went like this: sunglasses for Tony, a frown for John, cross-eyes for Terry, a nutter stare for Brian.

So simple, so effective. We just sat back and watched the tease start to tickle. We let the dog loose, let it slip the leash onto adverts and hoardings. We heard people asking 'Who is this dog? What does it stand for?' It stood for us, as people were about to find out...

I don't think there is too much point in explaining House of Love,
as I sort of wrote it as a self-explanatory tune. Every word was said and
sung 2 B heard and every statement was triple-checked and
double-triple-checked so that it was all to the point and clear.
I just pray that H.O.L. has been planted in the minds of everyone who
heard it and this world will become...

Heaven On Earth

HOUSE OF LOVE

It had to begin somewhere, and this was it.
Our first single, first hit, first video. First bite of the cherry.
Tasted good...

TONY: 'I wrote House of Love with Israel in mind because Israel
has got all the problems of the world within it. The troubles with religions,
the racism thing... it's all there, so I wrote that song based on Israel -
and it was Number One there. So I thought "Yeah, I do know what I'm
talking about. I know what it's like." It was wicked
to have a hit out there.'

BRIAN: 'My earliest memory of House of Love is of Anthony trying to sing
this bit, man, something like "the hills will crumble."
It was a good line, as it goes, but awkward to fit into the song.
Anthony couldn't do it, so it never made it. I felt like a pop star at the time;
there I was, in a studio, singing a song. I took the tape home,
played it to my Nan.'

TERRY: 'The video was just a laugh. It was cheap, but it was funny.
We were pushing each other to get in front of the camera.
They were going "Get into it!" and, like, we'd never made a video before.
We didn't really know what to do. We were just standing there
in front of the camera with the music playing. Looking back
now, it was a bit dodgy.'

JOHN: 'I was roofing at the time, and Anthony used to come round and tell
me he was doing music. He goes "D'you wanna help me do it?" I said "Yeah, alright."
We were in this really two-bob studio down in Blackhorse Road.
Bark studios it was called, as it goes. Bit poxy, it was, but we got the
idea for House of Love in there.'

From silence to screaming. House of Love did that for us. Smash Hits,
Top Of The Pops, Top Ten. And the weird thing is, you don't feel any different.
You can't really take it all in; is that us on TV and in them magazines?
It was, but it seemed like somebody else. Unreal.

EAST 17

GOLD

EAST 17

'Do not get involved
in materialism, for
an ism is a boundary,
and boundaries are
limited and limits
cannot be attached
2 spirits, 4 spirits
are free.' TONY

'GOLD is a song about
non-materialism - we used
gold as an example, as it is
recited in the Bible as an
object which is expensive,
and is something we really
don't need.' BRIAN

8

GOLD

WEDNESDAY, SEPTEMBER 30, 1992.
Westbridge Studios, Battersea, South London. Random thoughts
about our second video. Early start, late finish. Stale coffee in
plastic cups, crap catering, fags, females, hanging around.
Waiting, waiting, waiting. Such glamour! We could feel the devil
within us, but we looked like angels...

TONY: 'Gold. A non-materialistic point of view. Don't worry about
your car, your house - the size of it - your clothes. Your jewellery...
don't fret over it. It's not really important. In a hundred years
from now, it'll rust. It will be dust, but you'll still be alive.
For life goes on, but the form changes. I believe in
the message that I put in my songs.'

JOHN: 'Making the video for Gold was very tiring, but good fun.
The best part of it all for me was near the end of the day, when they
let us loose on the set. We sort of demolished the place, really,
which was a right laugh. You know, they go to all the trouble of getting
together all this weird stuff for the video - like this big polystyrene
statue of a dog - and then let us rip the place up. Nice one....'

BRIAN: 'It was weird - especially when you have to put on strange
plastic wings that have been sprayed gold and are held on by a piece of
white elastic. What's that got to do with the price of fish? But that's videos
for you; you do a load of strange stuff, mostly not even in the order of
the song or anything, and then you see the finished video and it looks
great. Best not to think too much about it. Just do it.'

TERRY: 'I had the runs that day, as it goes. There was some cook there,
man, and he made up some sauce thing, some spicy stuff that went
on these carrots, and it gave everyone the runs. So I was on a bit of a
downer because I just felt ill. I thought I was going to pass out.'

We don't need it - do we...?

DEEP

Telephone numbers. Deep sold enough copies in the UK alone to become one of them: 250, 000. THAT'S A QUARTER OF A MILLION SINGLES! In other words, one person out of every couple of hundred or so you see anywhere and at any time in the UK has got the record. Stupid, ain't it?

BRIAN: 'It's my favourite song of ours, to this day. It's been the most sorted tune of the lot, and I always knew it would be. Funnily enough, it was the first song I ever sang for the group.'

TERRY: 'We had a good dance routine to it. I really enjoyed performing it, and it used to make me laugh the way that people would scream when they watched Brian, Tony and myself doing it. You know, we were only dancing! It's definitely one of the best tracks on the album, and we even got a few friends in on the video! Love it... great.'

JOHN: 'About four of our mates appeared in the video with us, in all that army combat gear, but the rest of the geezers - about 20 of them - we didn't know. There was this one bird in a red hat kept on pushing in front of me. I thought she'd just joined the group or something, know what I mean?'

TONY: 'Aaah, Deep. A sexy, slinky kind of a song to get people going a bit. A slow groove, a gentle beat; it worked for me.'

And, lo! A new poetic coupling had entered into the vocabulary:

'REST UPON MY CHEST'

SLOW IT DOWN

People are always in a hurry. They've got this to do, that to do - and never enough time to do it in. Deadlines: they'll kill you. Loving, living, working, playing... why the rush? Where's the panic? That's what Slow It Down was all about. So take your time, do it right, think it through. Get on with your thing in your own sweet time. Chill, relax. To hell with the clockwatchers. Understand?

TONY: 'I've been writing songs since I was 14. I've been into philosophy and poetry, so songs ain't no problem. And I know what it is I want to say, so I just keep doing it in different ways. It's good for me to see that time, the last few years, have now actually amounted to something. As time goes on, it becomes clear what has happened, because you've got your own dreams about what might happen. But reality and dreams are kind of like a compromise.'

EAST END 17 BOYS WEST END GIRLS

BRIAN: 'For a band like us, doing the sort of music we do - which doesn't touch on anything the Pet Shop Boys do, for us to do a song they've done, to cover it and still make it sound good our way, I think that's quite an achievement. It's flattering to know that you are capable of doing it.'

TERRY: 'West End Girls should end the speculation over whether we can actually do covers, you know, can we actually sing other people's melodies. There's no point saying, in the pop world, "get together" if we're not going to sing other people's songs. So we did it.'

JOHN: 'The Pet Shop Boys don't like our version. They had them on MTV and asked them what they thought. One geezer went "crap", and started laughing. And then the other geezer, the old one, goes "It's a brilliant song. Mind you, I wrote it. But their version's not as good as ours." Sad, innit?'

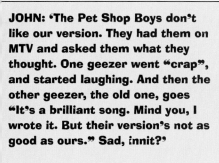

TONY: 'I can remember first hearing this song when our manager was looking after the Pet Shop Boys. I was just a kid at the time, imagining what it might be like to be in a band. Later on I tracked their manager down and kept on hassling him to help me. Now look what's happened; full circle.'

PIE AND MASH

Coming to a TV near you soon (it had better be in your house, know what we mean?) it's East 17 - THE MOVIE!

Yes, a ruff, tuff and wildly wicked film called PIE AND MASH. It's packed with all our videos plus a load of exclusive interviews and bits that could have ended up on 'the cutting room floor', as Denis Norden (whoever she is) might say. We're talking dance mixes, stuff nobody has ever seen before, stuff nobody has ever heard us say before. We'll be up for a poxy Oscar if we're not careful, luvvies...

TERRY: 'In less than a year, we've got like a feature film about us, showing all that we've done so far, and that. It's good, I reckon, just to see what's happened to East 17, and to see how the videos look. It's something to look back on when we're older, ain't it?'

EPK

Here's a problem for you. You're a Swedish geezer sitting in Stockholm, or a Japanese bird over in Tokyo or somewhere. And you're a journalist. You've got to write some stuff about us, and you've heard the records - but you need to know more. What do you do?

You pick up the dog and bone, make a call to our record company and go 'Can you send me an EPK, please?' (See note 1.)

'A what?' we hear you ask. 'An Electronic Press Kit, mate.' Allow John to explain: 'It's basically a video, right, of us sitting down and talking to the camera, telling people what we're about. It's about the group, behind the scenes and all of that. It's us having a laugh, and them filming it, so they can show people in the industry all around the world what we're really like. What are we like!'

We're like this; we're Londoners. So we got a few of our best pals in on the act to clue people in about life in the capital. We made a couple of calls to some associates to help give the thing some spice. You know the sort of people: a copper, a Beefeater, Princess Di, the Queen...

BRIAN: 'There's this bit in the EPK where Princess Di is listening to her Walkman and the Queen goes "stop that!" And Princess Di goes "I'm sorry - I was listening to East 17..." and the Queen goes "Who are they?" Di goes "Have a listen." So The Queen pops the headphones on, and Deep's playing. She goes "Oh, very nice!" Di goes "Yes, they're my favourite." And then the Queen goes "And they will be mine, too..." Good stuff, it is.' (See note 2.)

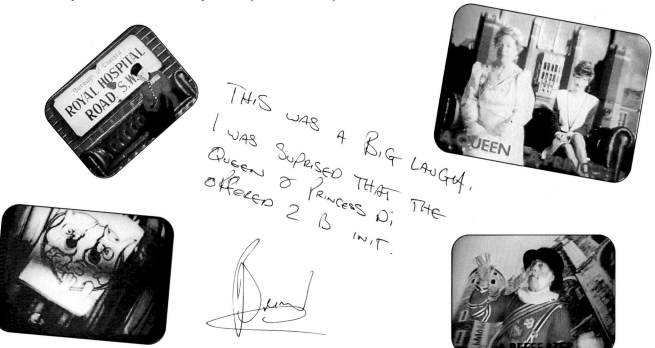

THIS WAS A BIG LAUGH. I WAS SUPRISED THAT THE Queen & Princess Di OFFERED 2 B IN IT.

Note 1: Don't try this if you ain't in the music biz - you won't get one.
Note 2: Brian is lying his head off. We used lookalike doubles for the EPK. Princess Di and The Queen were busy making a Chris de Burgh video.

We could've called our first album anything, but that's a stupid name, so we settled on Walthamstow. We ain't gonna upset or insult you by explaining why, but we will tell you a bit more about the place, and the people involved in the record, so you can fully get the vibe of where we're coming from...

TONY: 'My favourite place in Walthamstow is Bosch. It's part of a road that's derelict, and there's just an atmosphere around there. I've been hanging out there since I was nine or ten. I've just got so many memories of what's gone on there. I grew up there, with me mates. It's quite a landmark; the police know it, everyone knows it. It used to be an electrical store, Bosch, but it's closed down now.'
BRIAN: 'There'd be 60 or 70 of us chilling out there, getting moved on by the Old Bill, making noise - that sort of stuff. Bosch is a good place, if you want to hang out. If you go down there, there's all our names on the wall.'

JOHN: 'Walthamstow is just an average, everyday London borough. It's a hard, bad boy place. There's a lot of crime in Walthamstow, but you've got to mix with it all and just get across to people that it ain't worth it. What's the point? There's no need for it all. I know a lot of people involved with crime, but I don't mix with them a lot. But I do know them, and they're friends of mine... I just don't get involved in anything that they do.'

What's that they say about the inner city? Options to escape the ghetto are few: make crime pay, make it at sport, make music. Maybe we're the lucky ones...

TERRY: 'Your mates come up to you from school, and at school you used to be pretty bad - got kicked out of your lessons and all that - and you think they might take the mickey out of you because you've done a tune like House Of Love or something. But they don't. They respect you for it. Like, I saw my mate from school the other day, who I ain't seen for ages, and he was like, "Oh, what! Can't believe it!... You're a star now... " Freaks you, that does.'

JOHN: 'When I ain't seen mates of mine for ages and they come down, they go "You must be really proud of yourselves. You've made Walthamstow a much better place. You're doing it for Walthamstow." You don't actually think of them things, it's only when people say them to you that you realise maybe it's true.'

Enough, enough - you get the message; people like us from places like ours need to dream. We dreamed of making an album called Walthamstow. And when we did, this is what happened:

We recorded our songs and then gave them to some blindin' producers to mix and match and make those suckers groove. It was trial and error to get the right results; judge 'em for yourself.

We had our photographs taken a thousand times. Some looked good, others didn't quite cut it (cast your eyes to the left, dear reader, and you'll see what we mean).

We decided to launch the album in Walthamstow, where else, on February 15, 1993. We thought maybe nobody would show up. We were wrong; 3,000 people stood there in the rain waiting for us to make their day.

We went straight into the UK album charts at NUMBER ONE...

Cavern Records - The launch!

828 373-1

✳ Limited edition.
Includes FREE colour
EAST17
POSTER!

DEEP

V1
Turn the lights low
Put some music on
Let our bodies sing
Swing 2 the soft song
I feel ya heat
Its turning me
I wanna feel ya all night long so,
Come close as close as U can
I surrender youre so tender & tanned
I wanna toss I wanna tumble
feel & fumble, I wanna do it
till my belly rumbles
So lack back and ah!
Close your eyes and ah!
While I fiddle U can fantasize

Yeah
CHORUS
X4
Deep baby, deep deep down
Like sleep sugar, so rest upon my chest

What ya bodie wants
I got dis, whatcha need indeed
I'm gonna rock & this
I dream U scream & tighten ya hold
I tiggle in the middle as we giggle
In I go, Oh, deep & down deeper
like on cream
As I push I blow ya Emotions
You Xplode like, Dynamite
U got the fuse but to ya fuse I got the light
2 gether we swing
Shhh! I hear our soul's sing
A symphony, a lovers Harmony

Can U hear the harmony
REPEAT CHORUS

Deep 2

I'm gonna Kiss ya from ya head 2 ya toe
I'm gonna lick ya where you'd love
me to go, Yeah!
Oil ya skin within hold ya tight
Yeah I butter the toast
If U lick the knife
& take a shower?
Maybe bubble the bath
I'll wash yours, U wash mine
Yeah well love a good laugh.
I'll be the sponge
the sponge that wets U down
Then I'll be the towel upon
your naked body, wrapped around
& Then as a games come 2 an End
well start again
Again.

Repeat Chorus.

EAST17 ✳ WALTHAMSTOW

**This was originally going to be the cover of
our album. We didn't like it. The dog food
was happenin', though...**

All can happen
Dreams come true
Call out 2 love
It'll answer you
So don't cry
Smile
Let your ♥ speak
a white
& let the "light" of you shine thru

Don't be sad
Help is at your side
Don't be sad
Life can be short 2 live
Don't let tears fall
the love can hear U call
Its alright
The message (so) DID give

Walkin down a road
that goes no where
Walkin up a hill
That never ends
lookin for the answers
To all of the problems
The love that's in your ♥
holds the answer My FRIEND
@ V.3 @
All can happen
Dreams come true
Call out 2 love
It'll answer you
forget your troubles smile
let your ♥ speak awhile
let the light of light
thru"

Don't U worry
Its alright
Don't U worry
Child of the night
Cos in the mornin come
With the New day son
Love & Everlastin light

Don't U be sad (cos)
by your side
Holdin your hand, (sayin)
Its alright
Is the hand of love
Of beyond & above
Just Unlock the door 2 ya mind

The balloons went up when our album came out - one was found on the beaches of Normandy!

828 373-2
*
includes
HOUSE OF LOVE,
GOLD, DEEP &
SLOW IT
DOWN

PERSONAL APPEARANCE
CAVERN RECORDS, 165 High Street, Walthamstow E17
On Monday 15th February At 3:30pm

BRIAN'S NAN

CHART POSITIONS

So, this is the measure of success, and it blows us away to look at these chart positions. Here's your perspective on it all: a year ago we'd basically been nowhere. Now, the only place we haven't visited on these lists is South Africa.

The numbers show the highest positions we reached in the charts in each country.

HOUSE OF LOVE

Sweden	1
Israel	1
Denmark	4
Norway	8
Ireland	16
UK	10
Spain	40
Finland	1
Germany	6
Austria	7
Switzerland	15
Australia	5
France	8
Hong Kong	18

DEEP

Israel	1
Ireland	9
Denmark	7
Hong Kong	5
UK	5
Austria	7
Sweden	6
Finland	13
Holland	31
Switzerland	32
Germany	14
Australia	7

WEST END GIRLS

UK	11
Israel	2
Ireland	14
Denmark	22

SLOW IT DOWN

Israel	1
Denmark	12
UK	13
Ireland	12
Holland	50

WALTHAMSTOW

UK	1
Sweden	9
Switzerland	22
Germany	19
Austria	10
Ireland	22
Israel	4
Denmark	24
Norway	26
Finland	3
Holland	71
Australia	26

GOLD

Israel	1
Finland	3
UK	28
Sweden	2
Switzerland	35
South Africa	17

THE SCHEME TEAM

Whatever you do, you need a team around you to help make 'it' happen.
We couldn't have pulled this thing off by ourselves...
These are the geezers who have done the business for us. They're a right bunch of
sorts, but they're all we've got - and they are The Best at what they do.

JOHNNY BUCKLAND

John makes sure everything runs smoothly for us on a daily basis, and he sees
to it that we don't come to any harm. He's our security bloke and personal
assistant. That's the boring description; here's what we actually think about
the old duffer.

TERRY: 'He's a really good geezer, as it goes. He's like dad, really. Or mum.
You can tell him all your problems, and he'll sort them out. You have a laugh with
him, really. He's like someone our age.'

BRIAN: 'We trust John totally. Trust him with our money, our problems.
He's more like a mate, anyway, we don't see him as a work bloke. I call him
M Head, 'cos of the shape of his hair.'

JOHN: 'Security ain't about beating people up. You've got to be clever, got to
use your brain to get out of trouble before it starts. John's brilliant at that.
He's a blindin' geezer.'

TONY: 'Where East 17 go, John goes. He's a great bloke to have on your side,
and we'd be lost without him. He's a crap driver, though.'

This is Buckland working really hard in Australia. One of us took this smudge of
him, which makes a change since he's always snapping away at us with a poxy
camera and pretending he's David Bailey or someone. He's even blagged two
pages in this book for his photos, cheeky so-and-so!

MASSIVE MANAGEMENT

Ask us what day it is, go on. Here's your answer - today. In other words,
we don't know. Don't need to; Massive Management sorts out all of that stuff for us.
This mob organises our lives (from the moment we get up to the time we go to kip),
plans our career, advises us on how we should do things and, basically, totally
gets our act together. We'd probably completely hate the lot of 'em if they weren't
so bleedin'... good at what they do. Massive does what a management company
ought to: checks it out so we can get out there and do it.
By the way, it's Tuesday. Or possibly Friday.

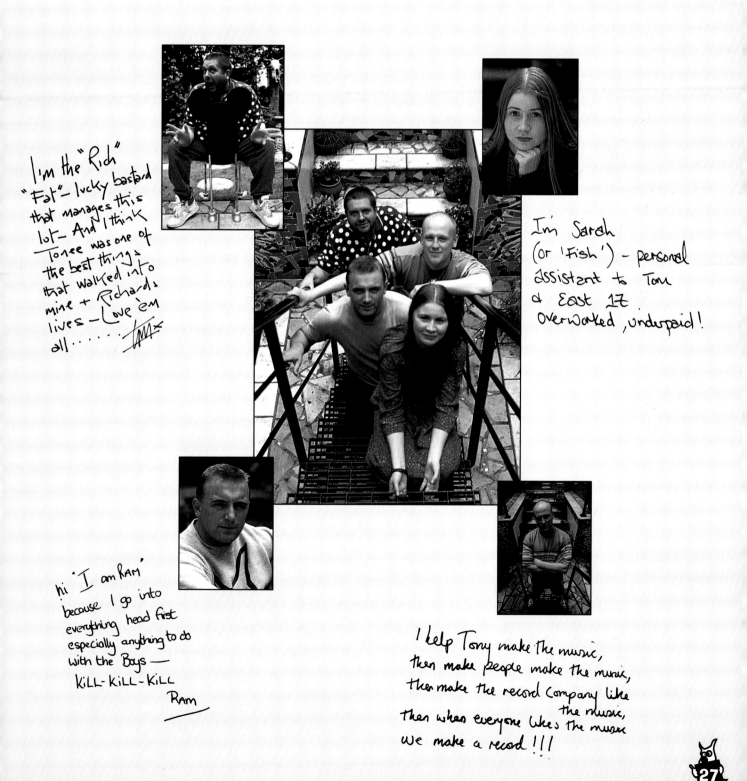

I'm the "Rich"
"Fat" - lucky bastard
that manages this
lot - And I think
Tonee was one of
the best things
that walked into
mine + Richards
lives - Love 'em
all....... TM x

I'm Sarah
(or 'Fish') - personal
assistant to Tom
& East 17
Overworked, underpaid!

hi "I am Ram"
because I go into
everything head first
especially anything to do
with the Boys —
KILL-KILL-KILL
Ram

I help Tony make the music,
then make people make the music,
then make the record Company like
the music,
then when everyone likes the music
we make a record !!!

LONDON RECORDS

Chairman: Tracy Bennett	Head of Marketing: John Reid	Marketing Manager: Keith Bennett	Press Dept: Juliet Sensicle	International Dept: Richard Evans Tracey Edensor Nick Bron

No record deal, no evening meal. We just invented that little poem to help you understand how important London Records is in the scheme of things. It's simple, really; if you don't sell records, you'll starve in this business. As it goes, we've not been hungry since Tracy Bennett, the Big Boss at London (thank you, Mr Chairman, sir) first heard us, loved us and signed us to the company. We work closely with him on our career, like when we're looking for producers and stuff, and he plans his moves with the help of John Reid and Keith Bennett. They work in the marketing department at London, which is where they decide when records get released. They also plan our campaigns (the advertising and all that lark) before and after a record hits the shops.

While all of that's happening, we'll be getting bugged every five minutes by Juliet in the Press Office. We like her, but she gives us too much work; she's always arranging interviews, competitions, photo shoots and stuff for us. Mind you, it is her job... And then, as if all of that ain't enough, we've also got to cope with Nick Bron in the International Department. This is where, you guessed it, they sort out our releases and what have you all over the world.

And there you have it - that's London Records. What are they trying to do, make us or break us?

FERRET AND SPANNER

Ain't got a clue why they call themslves what they do (maybe they've got things down their trousers) but we can tell you this - the people at Ferret and Spanner have 'been' on programmes like Top Of The Pops and had 'their' records played on Radio One more times than we've had hot dinners. You'll never see them on the box or anything, though. This crew are called pluggers, and what they do is convince the TV and radio bigwigs that they can't live without playing our stuff on their programmes. And they do it very well, so if you reckon you see or hear too much of us - blame them.

THE DESIGNERS

Paula Benson and Paul West are Bob Dog's mum and dad. They gave birth to him, designed him, like. And all of those East 17 logos you see on T-Shirts, posters, calendars, this book and all the rest of it - it's down to these two geezers as well. What they do for us is well important. They have to make our record sleeves and that eye-catching enough so that people look once, and then twice. Their company is called Form, and they're wicked. They do a really safe job. They're blindin', really - even if they are a pair of clever dicks.

THE PHOTOGRAPHERS

Weirdos. Just look at the state of them. But we do like them a lot, which is just as well since they've taken more shots of us than anyone else. Lawrence Watson did our first-ever photo session, for the House Of Love cover, and his partner Chris Clunn has done a load of our newer stuff. They also filmed a couple of our videos (Slow It Down and West End Girls) plus stuff for Pie And Mash - and they've both been doing photos of famous music types for papers and magazines for years. So they're totally on the case, and we'd rather have our smudges nabbed by them than anybody. They don't pull us about shouting 'exude, exude' or nothing. They just make us laugh, and they really do get the picture. They 'capture' whatever it is that makes us whatever we are with their cameras. Without being prats about it.

29

THE K-9 CLUB

When he's not skiving off and fishing, Mike Hrano (what a completely poxy surname) runs our official, international fan club. Looks a bit old to be a fan, but he set the K-9 Club up and he knows what he's doing. He's pulled it off (not ripped it off) for people like Bros, Seal, Pet Shop Boys, Status Quo and loads of other acts, so he ought to have a clue. He's the bloke who sees to it that our fanmail is opened, read and dealt with. He does a major job of it, too, 'cos he knows it matters to us - and that we'll do his kneecaps if he fouls up! As he's also a journalist, Mike writes loads about us, like the fan club magazines, tour programmes - plus he helped out with this book, but all of it is crap.

By the way, if you ain't a member of the K-9 Club, why not? Here's the address: The K-9 Club, P.O. Box 153, Stanmore, Middlesex, HA7 2HF. Send us a stamped, self-addressed envelope for the quickest response, alright?

COMPETITION!

ROLL UP! ROLL UP!

Get your pukka clobber here - and only the genuine East 17 article, madam. You've read the book (nearly), so now wear the T-Shirt. Thing is, it's a well exclusive, limited-edition bit of gear, which only punters like you can get hold of. If you fancy one, and we bet you do, fill out the form, snip it out or photocopy it, and do the necessary. Or else you'll be walking around topless for the rest of your life! On second thoughts...

And get this: the first 25 orders received will get the T-shirt - AND THEIR MONEY BACK - if they answer the following question correctly:

How many photos of Terry are there in this book?

HOW TO ORDER - Remember, you must enclose your payment, with or without your competition entry.

DON'T DELAY! SEND TODAY! WE ADVISE YOU SEND A PHOTOCOPY OR TONY WILL BE WELL CUT UP! (PTO)

✱✱THERE ARE .... PHOTOS OF TERRY IN THIS BOOK✱✱

	UK	Europe (inc. Eire)	Rest of World	Size (please tick)	Total Value of Goods
T-Shirt	£10.00	£11.00 DM 33.00	£12.00 US$ 24.00	L XL	

✱✱✱**PLEASE NOTE:** Price increases for Europe and the rest of the world reflect the additional cost of postage from the UK. The UK prices are inclusive of postage and packing.

METHODS OF PAYMENT:
UK£ - Cash, Cheque or Postal Order. IR£ - Cash or Postal Order. DM - Cash or Giro. US$ - Cash only. Members in UK and Europe may pay direct to our GIRO Account at Bootle, UK at any Post Office using Transcash (there may be a small charge). OUTSIDE UK cheques in UK£ (Sterling) may be obtained from any major Bank (or Post Office in Canada or Australia) near where you live.
✱Cheques/Postal Orders etc should be made payable to: THE K-9 CLUB (Account No. 5720567 National Girobank, Bootle, UK). PLEASE DO NOT SEND CHEQUES IN ANY CURRENCY EXCEPT UK£ (Sterling).
✱Alternatively, you may wish to pay by credit card:-

Please debit my Access/Mastercard/Visa/Eurocard (no other card accepted).

Card Expiry Date .... Card Holder No ....

Signed .... Date ....

I enclose my payment of .... Name ....

Address ....

.... Postcode ....

Please return this form and payment to: THE K-9 CLUB, PO Box 153, Stanmore, Middlesex HA7 2HF

TONY MORTIMER

1 Has been an estate agent, fishmonger, outsize-clothes salesman and a market trader.

2 Got beaten up at school for being a Rude Boy and wearing brogues.

3 Likes loose-fitting clothes which give him freedon to move.

4 Described Terry as 'a quiet boy' when they first met, and Brian as 'painfully loud'.

5 Has got a weird oven like a table in his kitchen.

6 Didn't own a record player until last year - and then gave it away.

7 Was born in Stepney on October 21, 1970.

8 Hates people taking advantage, interviews, politics and loads of other things.

9 Carries a tiny book of religious teachings and proverbs with him.

10 Has green eyes.

11 Doesn't have a nickname, other then Ant, but will answer to 'Painfully Thin'.

12 His first purchase as a record buyer was the entire Prince back catalogue, except for the Black album.

13 Has got the most bizarre, incredibly high-pitched laugh at times.

14 Is happy being on his own, doing his own thing, but gets bored quickly.

15 Has no heroes or heroines other than Jesus Christ.

16 Is easily influenced. Everyone has had an influence on him.

17 His greatest fear is that God doesn't exist.

But I know He does cos We are U & Me

Tonee ⟶

If U want 2C the view from the Mountain Top First U have 2 climb the mountain. Faith Is the Ladder

BRIAN HARVEY

1 Describes himself as loud, arrogant, short, annoying and ugly.

2 Is inspired by jackswing and thinks Guy is a kickin' band.

3 Uses the little spare time he has to go and hang out with his old mates in Walthamstow.

4 Had only been abroad once, to America, before East 17. Unless Butlins in Southend and Great Yarmouth count.

5 Has lots of mates and would like to say he has lots of cash. But he hasn't.

6 Wet himself at the age of 11 while riding on the top of a double-decker bus.

7 He has blue eyes.

8 Was born in North Middlesex Hospital, London on August 8, 1974.

9 His favourite drink is a bottle of Sol from any pub.

10 His hobbies are mixing records, drawing and answering the phone.

11 Reckons John Hendy is a good geezer, really.

12 Says anyone can dance; it's just a question of listening to the music.

13 Worked in sweet shop when he was young and was a plumber before East 17.

14 Refuses to walk under ladders, over three manholes or do anything else that might bring bad luck.

15 Admits that Love Me Tender by Roland Rat Superstar was the first record he bought.

16 Says sex, fame and money make him happy.

17 His worst habit is listening to what people tell him.

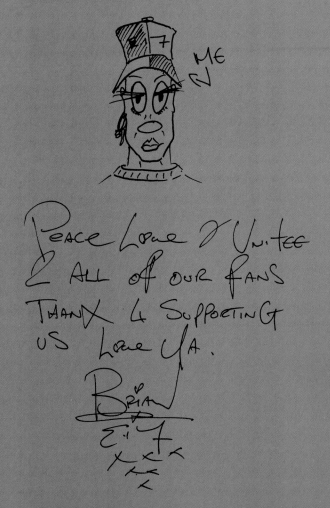

ME

Peace Love & Unitee 2 All of our Fans Thanx 4 Supporting Us Love Ya.

Brian
E17
x x x
x x
x

TERRY COLDWELL

1 Goes into a trance when he dances and thinks about nothing.

2 Likes hanging out at Cavern Records and Record Village in Walthamstow.

3 Hates all heavy metal music but doesn't mind Axl Rose.

4 Would dress like he does whether he was in East 17 or not.

5 His starsign is Cancer and he was born on July 21st, 1974, at Highbury & Islington Hospital in North London.

6 His favourite drink is a strawberry milkshake from McDonald's.

7 His hero is Scarface, because he was ruff, tuff, wicked and wild.

8 His greatest fear is John's bald head.

9 The first record he ever bought was Ossie's Dream by Tottenham Hotspur FC.

10 Reckons his good points are his muscles, his dancing and the way he dresses.

11 He finds it almost impossible to get out of bed in the morning.

12 He first performed live doing a Tarzan impression at a Butlins Holiday Camp competition when he was 11. He didn't win.

13 Used to be a paperboy, printer, builder, factory worker and bacon seller.

14 Dislikes shaving, cutting his toenails and the Queen.

15 Has brown eyes.

16 Enjoys movies with Jack Nicholson, Eddie Murphy or Whoopi Goldberg in them.

17 His dream night out involves naked girls dancing in the rain with scarves around their necks.

Thanks 2 all of our fans.
2 Everyone who has helped,
our manager, John buckland,
and Tony, John, brian, And
Many Many more people.
love & PEACE 2 ALL
thankyou
love
Terry
X E. 17.

JOHN HENDY

1 He reckons Arnold Schwarzenegger can't even talk properly, let alone act.

2 He says Levy is frightened of big crowds, screaming and noise.

3 He wants to learn how to play the saxophone.

4 When he was five years old, he dressed up as the Tin Man for a carnival.

5 East 17, Walthamstow, fast cars, nice women and his family make him happy.

6 He doesn't think he's got any good points.

7 He was born on March 26, 1971, in... Barking.

8 He once knocked himself unconscious while playing football. Jumping to head a ball, he missed and hit the goalpost instead.

9 He is not in the slightest bit superstitious, cross his heart.

10 His biggest fear is Brian's breath.

11 His favourite drink is Coke or Bacardi and Coke.

12 Has blue eyes.

13 Left St George Monoux School in Walthamstow six months early to become a chef.

14 His worst habit is biting his nails.

15 The first time he saw Brian, he laughed at him but thought he was alright.

16 His hobbies are playing football, collecting CDs and music.

17 He has a scar on his lip caused by his teeth going through it years ago when he skidded on ice and fell over.

Lots of love to our fans- making us what we are now. Thank you all
Peace

AROUND THE WORLD

You get tired of travelling about and that, but none of your mates have done it. It's a once-in-a-lifetime chance, really, getting to see all the different countries. Australia, Japan, New Zealand, Taiwan, Hong Kong... it's kind of hard to believe you're actually in all those places, but then you look around and there's John Buckland, with his camera out, snapping away to remind us all that we really are somewhere special. Somewhere you never really dreamed you'd ever get the chance to be. It's all a long way from Walthamstow, but here's the proof...

Quick, pile on for the photo. Smile, cheese.

This is me trying to find our car outside the hotel in Singapore, but I think all the fans have hidden it.

John with his familiar hand signal - Somewhere in Count Drocula's coffin. Look out Mr Photo Man Count Johnny Is gonna getcha!

ANOTHER MILLION WE'VE EARNT

HURRY UP IM HUNGREY MAN.

At the Singapore Cannibal Hotel.

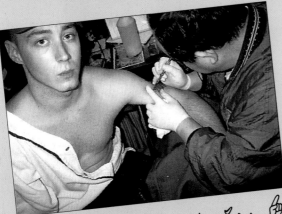

here I am in hong kong having  a tattoo done - looking very calm

Ouch!! Dont touch its  still scabby.

How COMES WERE NOT  IN THIS MAG?

Tonee 'Can someone help me with my  Coke can please?' John - '✳⊚!!? off mr photo-man?

The Posse, bang your dead,  HA, HA HA.

 Just finished a photo shoot for an Australian kiddie mag ☆ rare chance to get Big John in for one of our family shots. John & Terry run out of clothing ideas & decide to buy the same top twice.

 Is it a bird? Is it a phone? no its  Condom - Man,

☞ " I'm sure the Hotel was here last time I came wiv' bros'-Bros' ex-tour manager/mum—
  Johnny 'HIM' Buckland

☞ I saw a shark & it was this big, honest.

☜ This is me wiv' "nobody to play with" Tee hee!

🖐 Hawaii, what more can I say! Sun, Sea, Sand, women, absolutely great.

The water is bloody cold out here in maui, but the sun is bloody hot ☞

42

THE PAST

Check out these photos closely. Here we are, really not very long ago, looking
pretty much like we do now. We were a bit younger then, didn't have a record deal at the
time - never mind a hit - but there's no mistaking it's... us! Yet people clock us these days
and keep asking that same old question: has success changed you?
Our answer is this: of course it has, and of course it hasn't.
Sure, we're better known now, got more money, been more places but, inside, it's like it
always has been. We still hang out with our old mates in the old places - we just
have less time to do it. We still wear the same clothes, only now we can afford
the real McCoy, not just cheap imitations. And life is still hard, but in an
easier kind of way. That's how it is, believe it or not.
The same but different...

Who Stole
My Innocence?
Or have
I matured?

the hairstyle is the
same. - I grew a
goaty

WHAT A
XXXXXXX STATE
EH

'then' we had loads
of time off and we
looked rough. 'now'
we have no time off
but we look a lot
better.

44

THE FUTURE

As the cabbie might say to his latest fare -
where to now, guv? What's next for East 17?
Crystal balls ain't our thing, but we reckon it should
go something like this...

TERRY: 'A new album, which we're going to start
recording, followed by a full live tour some time next year,
probably March or April, when the record comes out.
We learned a lot of things off the first album, so we
know much more about what to do and how to
get what we want. We feel really positive about
the future, as it goes.'

JOHN: 'We're hoping that we'll have more hits, get more
sleep and just carry on doing what we've done so far
but in a better way. I think there's going to be a lot of
different changes within the band, too. Changes in
physique, clothing and musicwise. I reckon we're going to
be a lot more grown-up and professional.'

BRIAN: 'America. We'd love to bust the place open for
ourselves. Whether or not that happens, we know that everyone
is waiting for our next album - because the second album
is really the one which judges whether you're going to be a
success, or whether you're going to be a flop.
If you want my opinion, our new stuff will be even
more blindin' than the old.'

TONY: 'My thing is my message. I just want to keep
spreading the word. I'm a creator, and I believe that inside
us is this need to strive for perfection - and we're far
from perfect yet. There's so much work to do, and
when it's done, then I'll be happy. So I'm not stopping
with this or giving up or resting. I'm young, you know
what I mean? I can handle it...'

THANKS AND CREDITS

Once upon a time a skinny poor youth looked a fatter, richer man in the eye and implored, 'When will I be famous?' 'Not yet,' smiled the porkier one. 'Not until you get a group around you - then I will wave my magic wand.' The thin lad heard these words and understood. 'I'll bleedin' do that, then,' he cried to himself, and fearlessly set forth into the wilderness of Walthamstow to seek out some other trainee heroes. He searched high and low, past the Greyhound Stadium, along the High Street, through the derelict landscape until - one by one - he found what he had been looking for. Three (street) wise boys. He knew they were the right allies, that fame and fortune would soon be within their grasp. 'Wanna be in my gang?' he whispered to them. Yes. Yes. YES! The lithe leader fought his way back through the throbbing, naked city, found the wealthy guru once more and, panting, declared, 'Right, you fat git - do your stuff.' The tubby 'fairy' godfather, languishing in his opulent lair, sighed and then grinned. 'Alright, mate,' he nodded. So it happened that East 17 were given the keys to the kingdom of pop. And they WILL all live happily ever after. But not before they say:

TA!

Tom Watkins, Richard Stannard, Sarah Hollis
and Ram for services beyond...
Paula Benson and Paul West for designing
and pulling together this book.
Mike Hrano for asking the questions and
writing the answers.
Lawrence Watson and Chris Clunn for
pointing it in the right direction.
Rob Shreeve and Ríona MacNamara at
Virgin Publishing for the crazy deadlines.
To YOU for reading this, buying our gear
and supporting us.

AND THAT'S ABOUT IT REALLY...!

First published in Great Britain in 1993 by Virgin Books, an imprint of Virgin Publishing Ltd, 332 Ladbroke Grove, London W10 5AH. Copyright © 1993 East 17 Touring Ltd.
This book is sold subject to the condition that it shall not, by way of trade or otherwise, be lent, resold, hired out or otherwise circulated without the publisher's prior written consent in any form of binding or cover other than that in which it is published and without a similar condition including this condition being imposed on the subsequent purchaser.
A catalogue record for this title is available from the British Library. ISBN 0 86369 788 7.
Design by Form. Photography by Lawrence Watson and Chris Clunn. Printed by Proost, Belgium.